Blooms In Verse

Neha Raja

BookLeaf Publishing

India | USA | UK

Presentation by *BookLeaf Publishing*

Web: www.bookleafpub.com

E-mail: info@bookleafpub.com

ISBN: 9789358317992

First edition 2024

DEDICATION

Dedicated to my loving and hardworking mom, my funny and amazing dad, and my playful dog, Sammy.

ACKNOWLEDGEMENT

I would like to thank my parents for supporting me through this journey and BookLeaf Publishing for making my dream come true. Thank you.

PREFACE

This is a book about flowers, fun facts about them, and how they look. Cuddle up in your little nook and hook onto this interesting book. Don't be shook, but this one is a one you shouldn't overlook. This is what you took, not one that teaches you how to cook. Unless you mistook, you will now start your journey down the brook.

Bluebonnet

It is Texas's state flower,
But from the sun it never cowers.
Instead, it stands above like a tower,
Every minute and every hour.
The hillsides it overpowers.
Making everyone less sour.
The blue petals are never dour,
But like little water droplets falling from the
shower.
The plant makes a nice bower,
Where tiny insects like to devour.
The bonnet, you must empower,
To grow you must allow her,
Otherwise you might get an angry glower.
So next time take a minute and don't scour,
And admire this beautiful flower.

Tulip

The next one is a tulip,
A flower we should definitely not skip.
Shaped like a tea cup, the one you sip,
Or for biscuits to make a nice dip.
One by one the layers you can strip.
It is a pretty flower, from the bottom to the tip,
Which is a part that some people like to nip.
It likes to catch the water's drip.
But sometimes it lets it slip.
Its beauty is a curse, because some people like to
go snip, snip
While other people are unkind and just rip.
It looks good on a clip,
Or on a hula dancer's hip.
Although, the long leaves and stems might give
us a little whip,
It is great that we have this flower in our grip.

Rose

The USA's national flower is a rose,
And in Hunger Games, President Snow's.
Put on graves to convey one's woes,
Or a symbol of a kiss that blows.
Some people like to use it to propose,
And others like it to fill their meadows.
Some like the scent to fill their nose,
While others just like to watch it grow.
If you're lucky it might pose,
And put on a little show.
On the contrary, tantrums is does throw,
Because of their little thorns on their elbows.
Different colors it arose,
But red is the color that most people chose.
All are pretty and that, no one can oppose.

Marigold

The next one is a marigold.
The bright yellow color is very bold.
The texture is soft and velvety when you hold.
In many places the flower is sold,
To add color to your household.
Besides from being a charmer, behold,
It can grow pretty well in the cold.
The flower is manifold,
And although we see it a lot, it never gets old.
A lot of times you might want to scold,
The bugs leaving your flower's leaves holed.
It has a large threshold,
And by its uncanny scent, mosquitos it can
withhold.
Despite, its many immunities, it can not dodge
leaf mold,
But it is an extraordinary flower, all told.

Orchid

A common favorite is an orchid,
A lot of them are found in Madrid.
Although it might be a couple quid,
I shall most certainly not kid,
When I say that this is one that will open your eyelid.
Famous for the symmetry, like a grid.
Bends over a bit like it wants to be hid.
Many dark purple, like ink from a squid.
They take advantage of her beauty, they did,
Selling her like on an auction where buyers should bid.
Sometimes people don't care for her and she is bound to skid,
Kept in the middle of the table with no water, she slid.
That's why people who take advantage of her should be forbid
And she should be left in the wild, untouched, not kept under a lid.
This elegant flower deserves all her troubles to be rid.

Lilac

A color and a flower is a lilac,
A flower deserved to be on a plaque,
With its elegance from front to back.
It like to be timid, but is needs to flack,
It has a beautiful set of petals on its rack.
Not one day does it slack,
And turn a brown shade or black.
Some people like to chomp on it like a little
snack,
But its sharp bitter flavor might give you a little
smack.
It comes in bundles like it was squished into a
backpack.
The tiny flowers are one on top of another like a
stack,
And the heart shaped leaves are a little
something of a knack.
Their petals are like satin and are small like a
thumbtack.
4 petals like claws, ready to attack.
All in all this flower and color has gained fame
and made a big comeback.

Daffodil

My mum's favorite is a daffodil,
As if like clockwork, it comes to signal spring,
starting the drill.
The center opens up like it is about to shrill,
And the six petals fan out like a spill.
The quiet yellow color gives a feeling of thrill,
And its long leaves are the shape of a quill.
It grows on a meadow or a hill,
And it grows in clusters to fill.
Don't be fooled though, it has a secret skill,
Although it cannot kill,
If eaten it can make you very ill,
So while some people might say "Just pop it like
a pill!"
Don't mess around and quietly observe it from a
window sill.
The odd flower makes you think different
thoughts, it will,
So just believe that your wishes are the flower's
to fulfill.

Lily

A name and a flower is a lily.
It loves the warmth dearly,
But if there is none it might get a bit dreary.
They go dormant when it gets chilly,
And likes to grow where it is hilly.
It is cute like a filly,
And it's a good dilly.
Although it is pretty stilly,
The beautiful colors can range from a paper
white to a red chili.
But sometimes, the bright yellow might look a
little shrilly.
The petals look like tongues sticking out to be
silly.
The sizes can range from big to mini,
And a lot of times it makes people giddy.
It is fragile though, and fungi is its heel of
Achilles.
So stop to take a look at this flower even if you
are busy.

Lotus

The lotus is my dad's number one.
After June the lotus season has begun,
And only in August it is done.
It is sacred in India and Thailand and is valued a
ton.
Although it doesn't need soil, it loves the sun,
It is round shaped like a bun,
And with many petals it is spun.
The gradient on the petals are cool and fun.
The thick long stem is a stun.
The middle has curly legs, like it is about to run.
It gives off a nice feeling like one after a pun.
When it blooms it's as thought it is lifting its
hands to say it won.
Some people like to give it to someone special
like their son.
A lot of times the lotus is religious symbol like a
nun.
So love this special lotus otherwise to you other
people might shun.

Sunflower

"Sunflowers are my favorite!" a lot of people
once said.
Maybe because it is not bland like bread,
But a nice flavor like a yellow spread.
Unlike a thread,
The stem is thick like lead.
The flower has a large head,
Where the many petals are bred.
By the sun it is led,
And without the sun it would be dead.
The leaves are large and the edges look like it
was shred.
Not cup shaped, but circular instead.
The tiny petals it shed.
The flower doesn't give the feeling of dread,
But a sense that happiness is ahead.
This flower will always capture my thought,
awake or in bed.

Blossom

An orange blossom is the flower of Florida's
state,
Arizona's is a cactus blossom, with prickles so
straight.
Delaware's peach blossom is known to ward off
hate,
In Michigan and Arkansas, apple blossoms grow
at a good rate.
Missouri's hawthorn blossom has many seeds,
some more than eight.
Those are the states in the USA where the
blossoms pullulate.
In Japanese culture, the blossom petals are what
some ate,
And putting in tea is a nice trait.
They bloom on time, not one too late.
The petals fall in spate,
And the beautiful sight makes you wait.
To watch the blossoms, you need no mate,
Because you get mesmerized at the falling petals
with no weight.
The pink color is like the vibe of a date.
The blossoms should be valued as great.

Magnolia

Magnolia's grow in my backyard.
Elegant and graceful like a ballerina in a leotard.
They're delightful and looks like it should be put
on a card,
But some are marred.
In the white the pink is starred.
It's pink at the bottom, but the white takes guard.
The middle looks like a germ and is hard.
The trees it will bombard,
Some magnolias are barred,
Others are scarred.
The feelings of the magnolia's are never jarred.
The branches of the tree look charred.
A petal of it looks like a shard,
And are layered like a deck of cards.
You should give the flowers your best regards.

Jasmine

The jasmine is a flower very fair,
And is here for everyone to share.
In some cultures hear and there,
The flower is common wear,
Beaded on string and put on hair,
Or in perfume to put a nice smell in the air.
The flower is common, but its beauty is rare.
To its exquisiteness, nothing can compare.
In some cultures it is worth more than a
millionaire.
Some people think it is a little bare,
I think that those people are very unaware,
It might be simple, but to anything it adds a little
flair,
And is worth a good stare.
There one sentence we can declare,
This flower definitely does not bring despair.

Zinnia

A zinnia is round like a cupcake,
The ones that get round when you bake.
It is one you will not mistake,
For it is not opaque,
But it is like the middle of a rare steak.
Its brightness will keep you awake,
And your thirst, it will slake.
The stem is like a small thin snake,
The middle of the flower looks like a mini rake,
There are so many petals, it might give the
flower an ache.
Because of the petals, it looks as though it might
break.
Each petal is like a flake,
Layering on top of each other like algae on a
lake.
For the flower sake,
In keeping the flower safe, you should partake.

Hibiscus

The hibiscus flower is commonly put in food,
The petals, in tea it is brewed,
Or put in quesadillas to be chewed.
In the center, the pistol is ready to protrude,
But by its poisonous looks it could be construed.
As if it was cued,
On when it likes to be viewed,
Only in mid to late summers it likes to intrude,
And every year, it is to be renewed.
The color is never subdued,
Instead, the flower is heavily hued.
All of the shades it wants to include.
To conclude,
The hibiscus you shouldn't exclude,
And don't try to pick it off the tree and be rude.

Cosmos

Cosmos are the color of hot pink bubble gum,
The one that makes you say "yum!"
Few of them are the color of a plum,
In bright orange, there are only some.
They might seem familiar, but where are they
from?
Well some say, from your childhood drawings it
has come,
Probably the pink ones you use to draw for your
mum.
To grow this plant you don't need a green thumb.
Its bright yellow middle, circular like a drum,
That bees like to land on and thrum.
Its thin stems are like guitar strings you strum.
The price of the cosmos it not a big sum,
But it might be because the seeds are as small as
a crumb.
So don't be glum,
And listen to this charming flower hum.

Crocus

The crocus is similar to the tulip shape,
The flowers middle looks like the hands of an
ape,
Like it is coming out to scrape,
Or trying to escape.
Unlike Professor Snape,
It is sweet like a crepe.
They're soft and flow in the wind like a cape,
Or like a curtain's drape.
The purple is a beautiful shade like a grape.
It is not a scape,
But it has many leaves like the colors on a
serape.
The crocus is stylish, even when it's not in
shipshape.
Sometimes the bulb leaves a sticky residue like
tape.
You will probably gape,
If you see it in a landscape.

Forget-Me-Not

A popular flower is a forget-me-not
This flower might give one strong thought,
Or maybe a lot.
It might tie your stomach in a knot,
When you think of a memory you wish you had
forgot,
A memory that was always tucked away, in a
little slot.
A nice little gift, with a little jot,
To write some words that in your mind you got.
It might be small, but its value is more than a
yacht,
Because its love can never be taught,
And only by experiencing it, can the feeling be
brought.
People's lives end with a dot,
But the flower's meaning is forever, even if it
does rot.
Although the flower can be simply bought,
In your heart, it will always have a spot.

Poppy

A poppy is California's flower, you see,
Although, it might not make a good tea,
Or have a grow on a beautiful tree,
It still is a flower that gives me great glee.
There are not many petals, only a bit over three,
They are shaped like the letter c,
And it cups the middle of the flower, not letting
it be free.
The middle looks like little pieces of debris,
Or like a many tiny things that look like a flea,
It makes the whole flower right, even if it is like
a little black pea.
To understand this flower, you don't need a big
botany degree.
It shows respect to dead soldiers, like ones that
died on the day of the d,
Or to place on tombstones for thee.
Although, some people might disagree,
I think the poppy is heaven's key.

Daisy

The daisy is the one I like to view,
Because there are not only a few,
But it grows together, in a crew.
A daisy is a flower that is actually two,
The middle is a yellow flower, which petals are
like dew,
The outer is filled with bright white petals,
similar to glue.
They are pretty simple and are like the ones you
drew,
Or the ones you see on bottles of shampoo.
Picking it is something people should not do,
I used to think it was cute and pick it too,
But it belongs in a field, not in a stew,
Or to heal a person with the flu.
It is a symbol of love, so there is someone you
might give it too
But really think, who?
I just know that it will always be there for me
and you.

Lavender

The lavender gives me a feeling of excite,
Its purple color is vivid and bright,
And some are the color of the night.
In the field there are many standing upright,
Soaking in all of the sun's light.
It is free like a kite,
Flowing in the wind, in flight,
Up in the air at a great height.
When they grow in long rows it is a pretty sight,
It calls to you as if to invite.
They are packed really tight,
But they never fight,
Because their nature is too polite.
The smell it gives is a great delight,
And I know for me, this flower is right.

www.ingramcontent.com/pod-product-compliance
Lightning Source LLC
Chambersburg PA
CBHW071246140726
47996CB00007B/2773